The Age of Discovery
1400–1600

IN THE SAME SERIES

Austin Woolrych
England without a King 1649–1660

E. J. Evans
The Great Reform Act of 1832

P. M. Harman
The Scientific Revolution

A. L. Beier
The Problem of the Poor in Tudor and Early Stuart England

J. H. Shennan
France before the Revolution

J. M. MacKenzie
The Partition of Africa

Stephen Constantine
Social Conditions in Britain 1918–1939

LANCASTER PAMPHLETS

The Age of Discovery 1400–1600

David Arnold

METHUEN · LONDON AND NEW YORK

First published in 1983 by
Methuen & Co. Ltd
11 New Fetter Lane,
London EC4P 4EE

Published in the USA by
Methuen & Co.
in association with Methuen, Inc.
733 Third Avenue, New York,
NY 10017

Typeset in Great Britain by
Scarborough Typesetting Services
and printed by
Richard Clay (The Chaucer Press)
Bungay, Suffolk

British Library Cataloguing in
Publication Data

Arnold, David
The age of discovery, 1400–1600.—
(Lancaster pamphlets)
1. Discoveries (in geography) – History
I. Title II. Series
910'.94 G95

ISBN 0–416–36040–8

Contents

Foreword

Lancaster Pamphlets offer concise and up-to-date accounts of major historical topics, primarily for the help of students preparing for Advanced Level examinations, though they should also be of value to those pursuing introductory courses in universities and other institutions of higher education. They do not rely on prior textbook knowledge. Without being all-embracing, their aims are to bring some of the central themes or problems confronting students and teachers into sharper focus than the textbook writer can hope to do; to provide the reader with some of the results of recent research which the textbook may not embody; and to stimulate thought about the whole interpretation of the topic under discussion. They are written by experienced university scholars who have a strong interest in teaching as well as an expertise, based on their own research, in the subject concerned.

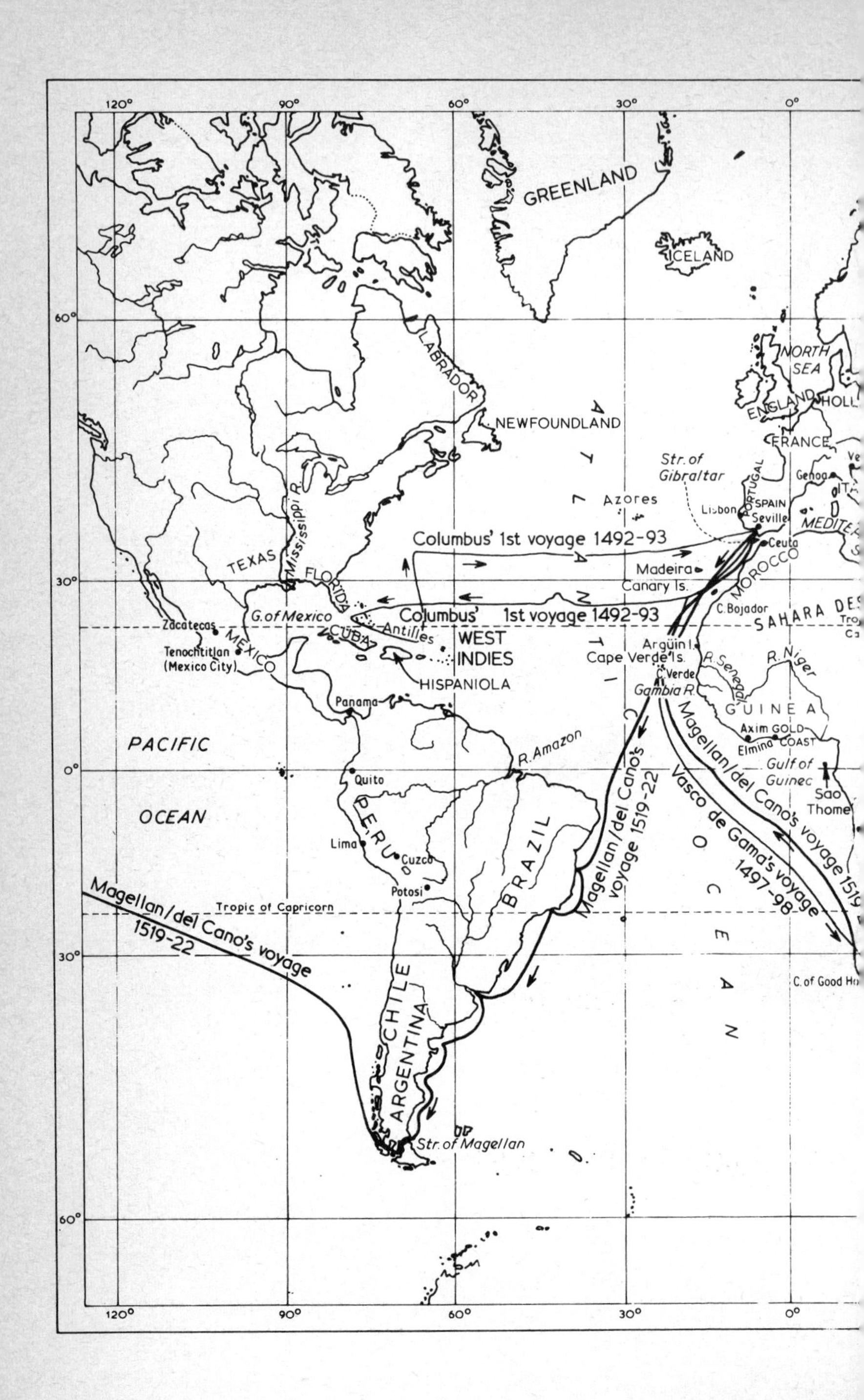
120°
90°
60°
30°
0°
GREENLAND
ICELAND
NORTH SEA
ENGLAND
HOLL
FRANCE
LABRADOR
NEWFOUNDLAND
Str. of Gibraltar
PORTUGAL
Genoa
Lisbon
SPAIN
Seville
Azores
Columbus' 1st voyage 1492-93
Ceuta
Madeira
Canary Is.
MOROCCO
C. Bojador
SAHARA DES
Mississippi R.
TEXAS
FLORIDA
G. of Mexico
Columbus' 1st voyage 1492-93
Zacatecas
MEXICO
Tenochtitlan (Mexico City)
CUBA
Antilles
WEST INDIES
HISPANIOLA
Arguin I.
Cape Verde Is.
C. Verde
Gambia R.
R. Senegal
R. Niger
GUINEA
Axim
GOLD COAST
Elmina
Gulf of Guinea
Sao Thome
Panama
PACIFIC
OCEAN
R. Amazon
Quito
PERU
Lima
Cuzco
Potosi
BRAZIL
Magellan/del Cano's voyage 1519-22
Vasco de Gama's voyage 1497-98
Tropic of Capricorn
Magellan/del Cano's voyage 1519-22
C. of Good Ho
CHILE
ARGENTINA
Str. of Magellan
ATLANTIC OCEAN

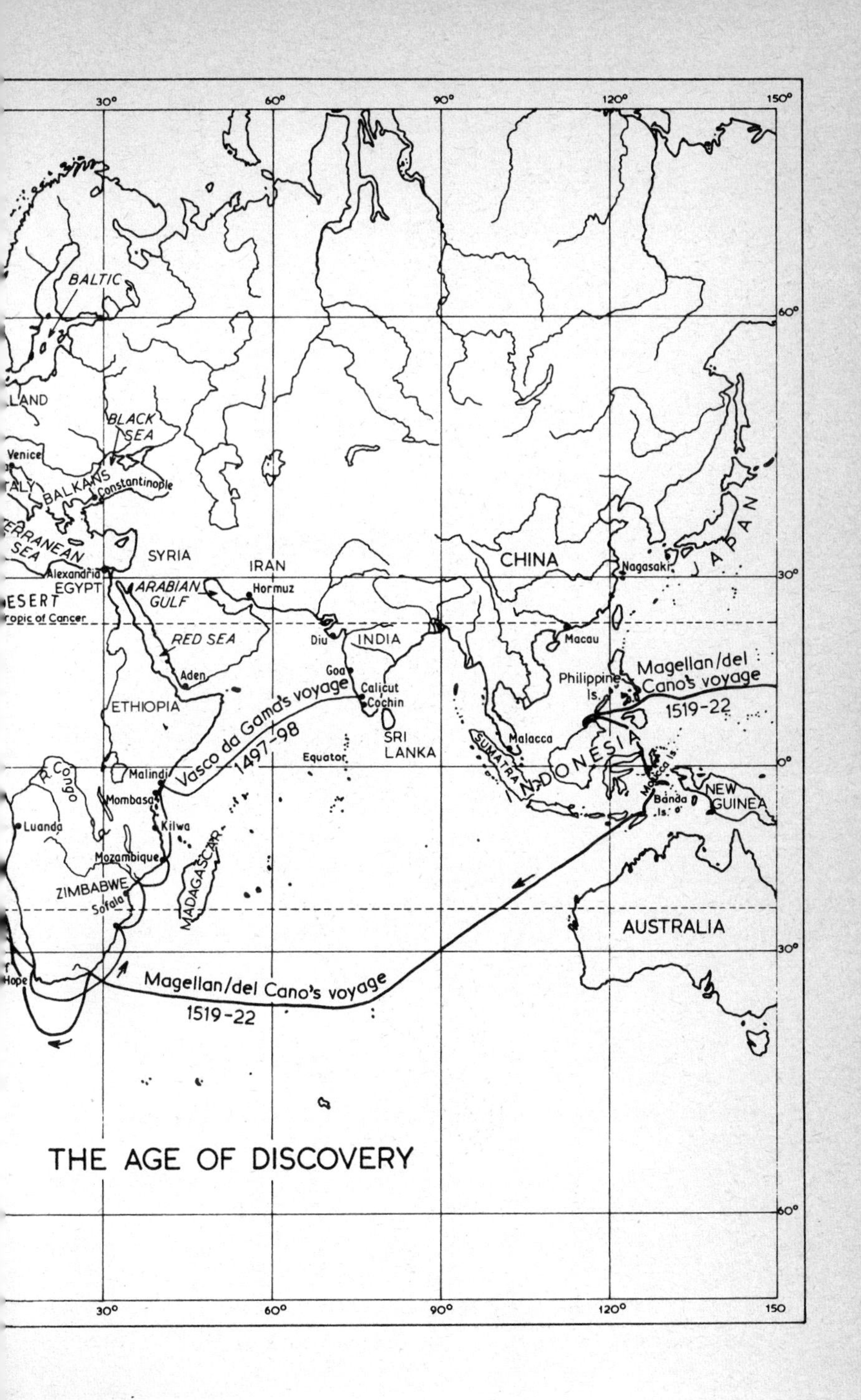

THE AGE OF DISCOVERY

The age of discovery, 1400–1600

Introduction

During the fifteenth and sixteenth centuries Europe's knowledge of the rest of the world underwent a fundamental transformation. In 1400 Europeans had, as their maps show, only a vague, and often totally mistaken, idea of what lay beyond their own shores. In the two hundred years that followed the continents drawn by Europe's map-makers developed, like growing embryos, from uncertain blobs into the readily recognized outlines familiar to us today. Only Australia, New Zealand and the North Pacific remained by 1600 either absent from the maps or imperfectly drawn. Many of the most significant discoveries were made in a breathtakingly short span of time. Within thirty years of Columbus's first trans-Atlantic voyage in 1492 the Portuguese had rounded the Cape of Good Hope and advanced as far as China and Japan. By 1521 the Pacific had been crossed and the world circumnavigated for the first time.

In themselves, long-distance voyaging and discovery were not new. Other navigators – among them Arabs, Indians, Chinese, Vikings and Polynesians – had accomplished spectacular trans-oceanic journeys before the Europeans of the fifteen and sixteenth centuries. But their achievements were forgotten and not repeated, or were never of more than localized significance. What was new about the Age of Discovery was the linking up, through exploration, of the oceans of the world into a single system of navigation and the way in which this mastery of the seas became the basis for the eventual extension of European influence into every inhabited continent. The growth of Europe's geographical knowledge was rapidly followed by the expansion of European trade and territorial control. By 1600 Portugal held a maritime empire from Brazil and West Africa to the China Sea. Spain's American empire stretched from Texas to Chile, and other Europeans – the Dutch, English and French – were becoming openly covetous of the Iberians' trading wealth and dominions.

How can we account for the rapidity of European exploration and expansion? Was the Age of Discovery in fact as sudden and as sweeping as it at first sight appears, or was it rather the outcome of forces long maturing within Europe itself? What were its motives, and why did Portugal and Spain pioneer European expansion? How did factors outside Europe affect the character of this expansionism? These are the issues with which this pamphlet is concerned.

Europe and the wider world

It is not easy from a present-day perspective to imagine a time when Europe was still a relatively isolated and self-contained society, with little knowledge of what lay beyond its own boundaries, and when the map of the world, so familiar to us today, did not exist. But until the discoveries of the fifteenth and sixteenth centuries such awareness as Europe had of the outside world owed more to myth and fantasy than to actual knowledge.

Among the more reliable sources of information available to fifteenth-century Europe were texts surviving from classical antiquity and more recent travellers' accounts. Ptolemy's *Geography*, written in the second century AD but only rediscovered in Christian Europe through a Latin translation of the Greek made in about 1406, was a compendium of geographical knowledge as it existed at the height of the Roman empire. While it provided a fairly accurate description of the nearer regions of Asia and Africa, it was an unreliable source for more distant lands and could give no clue to the existence of the Americas and other parts of the world unknown to the ancients. Among the most popular and influential of the works of travellers was the account of the Italian

Marco Polo who had journeyed across Asia in the late thirteenth century and visited the court of the Mongol emperor in China. Polo helped to establish in the European mind the idea of Asia as a continent of great wealth with advanced and powerful civilizations. His *Travels* were an inspiration to Portugal's Prince Henry 'the Navigator' and (along with Ptolemy) Christopher Columbus. But such sources had their disadvantages. The Mongol-ruled 'Cathay' (China) that was one of Columbus's objectives in sailing west across the Atlantic had long since disappeared, and late medieval Europe's deep conviction that the ancients were right in everything (except religion) inhibited a critical approach to their geographical texts and a spirit of practical enquiry.

However, deficient and out-of-date as Ptolemy and Polo might be by 1400, they at least provided a more dependable source of information than the myths, legends and spurious travellers' tales that otherwise shaped late medieval Europe's notions of the wider world. One of the most widely circulated works, and certainly no less influential than Polo, was Sir John Mandeville's *Travels*, an almost entirely fictitious account of the strange inhabitants (such as dog-headed men) and bizarre customs of the East. In the popular imagination there persisted, too, beliefs that ships venturing too far into unknown seas might fall off the edge of the world or perish in the boiling seas of the 'torrid zone'. Such fears were a powerful deterrent to exploration and practical investigation. But there were other fantasies – of the existence of 'lost' islands and a continent of Atlantis in the west, of a powerful Christian king, Prester John, ruling somewhere beyond the Muslim lands in Asia or Africa – which, however unrealistic, played a part in motivating the fifteenth-century voyages of discovery.

The same mixture of fantasy and half-truth was evident in the maps of the medieval period. In the earlier ones Jerusalem, as the spiritual capital of Christianity, appeared at the centre of a circular world with the known continents arranged symmetrically around it. These *mappae mundi* were of no practical use to navigators and travellers, nor were they intended to be. Later ones, influenced by Ptolemy, sketched in the northern part of Africa and the western regions of Asia with some accuracy, but were uncertain how far south Africa extended and whether the Indian Ocean was a landlocked sea. Of the Americas, Australasia and the Pacific there was no trace. The map-makers compensated for Europe's ignorance of the interior of Africa and Asia by drawing in rivers and mountains of their own invention and set fictitious or long-dead monarchs to rule over them.

Europe was not alone in its ignorance and isolation. The world in 1400 was divided into dozens of separate societies and civilizations with little or no contact and communication between them. Some, like the peoples of Central and South America, were entirely cut off from other continents. Others, like the great Asian civilizations of China and India, had wider connections, principally through trade, but these did little to pierce their basic cultural isolation and economic self-sufficiency. In part this isolation was a consequence of geographical barriers – seas, deserts, mountain ranges and dense forests. But it was reinforced by the absence of transport, communication and control which could fuse diverse peoples and regions into larger entities. Often, too, there was simply a lack of curiosity to motivate long journeys of discovery by land and sea.

China was a striking example of this. In 1400 its maritime technology was in many respects Europe's equal. It had regular trading relations with southeast Asia, and between 1405 and 1433 Chinese expeditions under Admiral Cheng Ho sailed as far as Sri Lanka and East Africa. At this time, or earlier, Chinese ships visited northern Australia and perhaps the Pacific shores of North America. But Confucian China held itself to be culturally and politically superior to its neighbours, whom it looked down upon as barbarians, fit only to pay tribute to the Chinese emperors. Cheng Ho's voyages appear to have been motivated by a quest for tribute and for luxuries and curiosities for the Chinese court, not by a desire to extend China's knowledge of the rest of the world or open up lasting trading relations. Trade and merchants occupied a lowly position in the Chinese empire: the contrast with Europe's increasingly assertive and prosperous merchant classes is an extremely significant one. Cheng Ho's expeditions were not followed up and China retreated again into self-imposed isolation at precisely the time the Portuguese were edging their way down the West African coast and beginning to seek a western route to the Indies.

Arab and Indian Muslim merchants operated a complex and extensive system of trade in the Indian Ocean, but they were content to restrict their activities to areas of known profitability and safe navigation. Although Arab ships had once traded directly with China, by 1400 they seldom ventured further east than the Indonesian islands In the southwest they did not pass far beyond Mozambique and Madagascar, where sailing conditions grew hazardous and trading prospects appeared unrewarding. Similarly, Arab sailors and geographers in the Mediterranean believed that beyond the coast of Morocco the Atlantic became an unnavigable 'green sea of darkness'.

In certain respects the Europe of 1400 seems particularly isolated and inward-looking, a civilization under siege and thus unlikely to take the lead in an age of exploration and expansion. The Black Death, the plague epidemic that swept through Europe in 1348–9, left economies battered and populations cut by a third or more. It was to take more than two centuries for the population of Europe to regain the levels of the mid-fourteenth century and, it has been claimed, it needed the mineral wealth of the Americas in the sixteenth century to revitalize Europe's economy. Climatic changes, too, contributed to the sense of a besieged Europe. In the relatively warm conditions that prevailed between the eighth and fourteenth centuries settlement and agriculture had been pushed further north and west. The Vikings had established colonies in Iceland, Greenland and reached 'Vinland' on the northeastern coast of mainland America. But colder conditions, heralding what has been termed 'the Little Ice Age', brought an end to this expansion. The southward advance of Arctic pack-ice cut off the northerly route to Vinland and threatened contact with Greenland and Iceland.

To the south, the Mediterranean, once the heart of the Roman empire, was divided between Christian Europe and its Muslim neighbours. In the west, in the Iberian peninsula, the emerging states of Portugal and Spain had succeeded in gradually pushing back the Muslims who had overwhelmed the region in the eighth century. By 1400 only Granada remained (and that as a virtual client state of Castile) until it, too, was absorbed in 1492 after a ten-year struggle. But although Muslim power was finally being expelled from the peninsula itself, the Portuguese and Castilians were to find it more difficult to carry their crusade across the Straits of Gibraltar and into Muslim North Africa. Portugal captured the Moroccan port of Ceuta in 1415, a date seen by many historians as marking the real start of the Age of Discovery, but attempts to extend this bridgehead met with little success. In 1437 Portuguese forces were decisively defeated at Tangier. Following the conquest of Granada, the Castilians established themselves at Melilla in 1497, but their further territorial ambitions in North Africa were thwarted first by the effectiveness of local Muslim resistance and later by the expanding power of the Turks.

At the eastern end of the Mediterranean, the Ottoman Turks were clearly in the ascendent in the fifteenth and early sixteenth centuries. Constantinople, the last remnant of the once mighty Byzantine empire, fell to the Turks in 1453. In 1516–17 they defeated the rival Muslim rulers of Egypt and Syria, the Mamluks, and extended their control over the southern shore of the Mediterranean. The Turks advanced through the Balkans, too, threatening Vienna in 1529. By origin nomads and horsemen from Central Asia, the Turks became heirs to Byzantine naval traditions when Constantinople fell, and became a formidable force in Mediterranean waters. Although checked in 1571 by the battle of Lepanto, off the Greek coast, the Turks remained firmly established in the eastern Mediterranean. Thus in the fifteenth and sixteenth centuries the crescent of Islam, curving from Morocco in the west, through the eastern Mediterranean and Levant to the Balkans and the Black Sea in the east, effectively contained Christian Europe and blocked its natural path of expansion into adjacent areas of Africa and Asia. The entrenched power of Islam made it necessary that any European age of exploration and conquest must first involve a dramatic leap beyond Europe's immediate boundaries.

It would, however, be a mistake to exaggerate Europe's isolation and internal difficulties. Despite religious animosity and periodic warfare, Christian Europe had learnt a great deal from the Islamic world, both through its preservation of Greek science and philosophy and through its transmission of scientific and agricultural knowledge and technology from as far away as India and China. The importance of this Islamic-Asian contribution to the European Age of Discovery will be discussed later in this pamphlet. Internally, taking the period AD 1000 to 1400 as a whole, there had been far-reaching economic and technological progress in Europe. Until the severe setback of the Black Death there had been a marked growth in population. Farming techniques had improved and contributed to greater agricultural productivity, especially in northern Europe. There had been an expansion of trade by land and sea, with increased activity not only in the Mediterranean but also in the Baltic and the North Sea and between northern and southern Europe. With the growth of trade and shipping had come major advances in banking and finance, especially in the cities of Pisa, Florence, Genoa and Venice in northern Italy. The underlying vitality of the European economy, and the search to provide it with more trade and new resources, created the fundamental drive behind European expansionism in the fifteenth and sixteenth centuries. However the forms which the movement took were shaped by influences that were not exclusively economic in character.

Spices and gold

The West's image of Asia and Africa today is very different from that which fifteenth and sixteenth century Europeans had. Rather unjustly, we now associate large parts of those continents with poverty, famine, disease and economic backwardness. They constitute part of what we call the Third World or the developing countries, and we contrast the affluent 'North' (including Europe and North America) with the impoverished 'South' (including India, China and Black Africa). But four or five centuries ago Europe saw itself as being in certain respects the poor neighbour of Asia and Africa. Europe formed its impressions of these continents not only from travellers' reports but also from the nature of their products. Gold, jewels, silks, carpets, tapestries, spices and porcelain suggested luxury, wealth and creative industry, and it was this image of Africa and Asia's riches that inspired the first European voyages of discovery.

In the late Middle Ages Europe stood at the end of two major long-distance trade routes. One, the spice trade, linked Europe to Asia; the other, the gold trade, connected Europe with Africa.

Despite periodic interruption by wars, invasion and the collapse of empires, there had been trade routes across Asia to Europe since Roman times bringing silks, spices, gems and other high-value commodities from China, Indonesia, India and Iran. The importance of the silk trade had declined with the development of Europe's own production, but Europe had no substitutes for Asian spices. They originated either in the Indonesian islands – cloves were grown in the Moluccas, nutmeg and mace in the Banda islands, pepper principally in Sumatra – or in Sri Lanka (formerly known as Ceylon) (cinnamon) and southwestern India (pepper). In Marco Polo's day spices, along with other goods, were transported by caravans overland through western Asia to the Black Sea and Levant. With the disintegration of the Mongol empire that route became too hazardous and by 1400 Arab and Indian traders conveyed the spices by sea to ports on the Red Sea. From there they were carried overland to the Mediterranean ports of Egypt and Syria where Venetian and Genoese merchants bought them for distribution and sale in Europe.

To us today spices might seem a curiously insignificant basis for such an elaborate and extended system of trade. Pepper is an everyday item of consumption and relatively cheap. We attach little importance to cloves, cinnamon and other spices. But in the fifteenth and sixteenth centuries spices of all kinds were in great demand in Europe. Their principal use was to give flavour to the stale or salted meat consumed in the days before there was adequate fodder to keep more than a few animals alive during the winter and when there were few vegetables, fruits and beverages available to give variety to the basic diet. Spices gave greater interest, too, to cakes, drinks and confectionery. The Crusaders' experience of spiced eastern food may also have encouraged a European taste for more exotic flavourings. Spices have often been classed as a luxury: Edward Gibbon referred to them as one of the 'splendid and trifling' products of trade with Asia. But it is clear that their use was widespread and not confined to the wealthiest classes of Europe and, as Europe's economy developed and its purchasing power increased, the demand for spices steadily grew.

For the merchants who dealt in them spices were a highly profitable commodity. The wealth derived from the spice trade was one of the economic bases for the rise of the Italian city states, Genoa and Venice in particular. Spices, moreover, were one of the few commodities to make such long-distance trading profitable. Their value was high relative to their volume – an important factor in the days before cheap, bulk transportation – and spices were sufficiently durable to survive the long journey and frequent transhipment.

Gold, the other major product of Europe's long-distance trade, was also more than a mere 'luxury' commodity. In addition to its use for decoration and display in churches, palaces and the houses of the rich, gold was required for Europe's coinage and expanding system of trade. As their commercial and financial activities grew, the Italian city states turned to gold as the basis for their currencies: Florence and Genoa minted gold coins from 1252, Venice from 1284. Even the poorer states of Europe, like Portugal, were eager to establish their currencies on the same prestigious basis. Europe also needed gold to lubricate its internal economy and to pay for trade with the East. Europe produced few commodities of its own that could command a market in Asia: instead it had to buy spices with precious metals. Silver was mined in Germany and Hungary, but Europe was poorly endowed with gold. Many mines which had formerly supplied gold were now exhausted; much gold had been lost to Europe through plunder and continuing trade with the East. There existed, therefore, a 'gold famine' in late medieval Europe, which was both a check on internal economic development and a powerful incentive to trade and exploration overseas.

During the late Middle Ages a small but significant quantity of gold reached Europe from West Africa. It was extracted by surface mining and panning in the Bambuk area of the upper Senegal River and at Bure on the upper Niger. A further gold-yielding area, Akan in present-day Ghana (the 'Gold Coast' of colonial times) was also becoming productive by the late fourteenth century, partly in response to European demand. From these sources in Black Africa, the gold was transported, usually in the form of gold dust, by local traders to towns like Timbuktu on the southern fringes of the Sahara. There the gold was bought by Arab and Berber traders, carried across the desert by camel caravans and then sold in North African ports to Genoese, Venetian, Catalan and Jewish merchants. In exchange for this West African or 'Guinea' gold – our term 'guineas' is a lingering reminder of the one-time importance of this source of gold – the trans-Saharan traders sold textiles, copper, salt and other commodities in demand south of the desert. Although before 1400 Europe had no direct contact with the gold-producing area, fairly accurate reports of its location filtered through Arab and Jewish intermediaries and excited European avarice.

Though the most spectacular, gold and spices were not the only commodities tempting Europeans to reach beyond their own shores in search of trade and wealth. Even as basic an item as corn was being imported from Morocco and from the Atlantic islands – the Azores, Madeira and the Canaries – once, during the late fourteenth and early fifteenth centuries, these had begun to be colonized and cultivated by European settlers. Sugar was even more closely associated with European expansionism. The cultivation and consumption of sugar had been adopted from the Arabs (another reminder of medieval Europe's debt to the Muslim world) and it had at first been grown in the Mediterranean islands and favoured parts of Sicily and Spain. But increasing demand encouraged a search for new areas of production. Sugar became a pioneer crop in Madeira and the Canaries, then, in the late fifteenth century, on the island of Sao Thome in the Gulf of Guinea, and later still, across the Atlantic, in Brazil and the West Indies. Fish, too, was being sought at ever increasing distances from the home shores of Europe, especially by the Portuguese off northwest Africa and in the North Atlantic. Dried and salted cod formed an important item of Portugal's trade with the rest of Europe.

A grimmer commerce, in slaves, was also developing. The expulsion of Muslims from the Iberian peninsula and the effects of the Black Death had left southern Portugal in particular thinly populated. A trade in black slaves had long accompanied the gold caravans across the Sahara to North Africa and it was extended to supply southern Europe as well. During the course of their early expeditions down the west African coast the Portuguese bought or captured slaves to provide labour for estates in Portugal and subsequently to meet the labour needs of the expanding sugar economies of the Atlantic islands. The association of European expansion and exploitation overseas with sugar and slaves, which was to be such a brutal feature of the seventeenth and eighteenth centuries, was thus already established even before Columbus crossed the Atlantic in 1492.

The economic drive behind expansionism was not, therefore, a search for markets for European goods. In Africa and Asia in the fifteenth and sixteenth centuries Europeans experienced great difficulty in trying to sell their own textiles and other products. The age of European industrialization and the mass manufacture of machine-made goods was still far in the future. Europe's quest overseas was for trade and for resources that could become part of the European system of trade. But the argument that expansionism was an outcome of developing commercial capitalism in Europe confronts us with an apparent contradiction. If economic motives were of such fundamental importance, why did Italy, economically the most advanced region of Europe, seemingly fail to play a significant part in the overseas expansionism of this period? Why instead did the economically more backward Portugal and Castile pioneer exploration and become the first European states to establish their empires overseas? The answer is a complex one, for a number of factors are involved. But it is important to note first of all that Italy did make a very considerable contribution to the Age of Discovery.

Italy

Partly because national identities and national boundaries were so uncertain in the fifteenth and sixteenth centuries European explorers and scholars, as well as traders, soldiers and seamen were able to move from the service of one country to another with relative freedom. This mobility, along with the newly-invented printing press, was important in disseminating information about the first voyages of discovery throughout Europe, despite some attempts, by the Portuguese in particular, to keep their findings secret. The Portuguese, indeed, as the first voyagers stood to lose most by the loss of information and personnel to other countries. Castile, by contrast, in part owed its rapid and dramatic entry into the field of exploration in the late fifteenth and early sixteenth centuries to outsiders, notably the Portuguese Magellan and the Italian Columbus.

Christopher Columbus is a prime example of the importance of mobility among the early explorers and of Italy's contribution to the Age of Discovery. Born in Genoa in about 1451, he subsequently settled in Portugal, married a Portuguese woman, and first offered his scheme for sailing westwards to China to the Portuguese court. Rejected there, he sought French and English support before eventually finding a royal patron in Queen Isabella of Castile. The career of John Cabot has many similarities. He, too, was Genoese by birth. Like Columbus, he tried in vain to interest several governments in his proposal for exploration in the western ocean until, following news of Columbus's return, Henry VII of England agreed to sponsor an expedition in 1496. Because Europe, unlike the unified empire of China, consisted of a number of states with different interests and ambitions, it was possible for adventurers and men of ideas to hawk their schemes in several countries if they failed to attract patronage in their home or adopted country. Conversely, state or royal patronage was essential to these early voyages. The costs and risks of providing and equipping ships for major expeditions were too great for an individual merchant or adventurer. Navigators needed, too, the political authority of a state to permit them to use its harbours and ships, to employ its sailors, to guarantee their rights to new lands discovered and to protect claims to territory and trade against the encroachments of other powers.

In return for patronage from Portugal, Spain or England, the Italians brought to the service of western Europe ideas and skills, particularly in map-making and certain techniques of navigation derived from the Italian Mediterranean. To some extent they also brought the learning of the Italian Renaissance, particularly a knowledge of recently rediscovered classical texts, like Ptolemy's *Geography*.

Some controversy surrounds the origin of the name 'America'

that came to be applied to the western continent. It has been suggested that it comes from Richard Ameryk, collector of customs at Bristol, who paid Cabot his official pension. But there is an older and perhaps more probable view that the name is derived from that of a Florentine businessman, Amerigo Vespucci, through whose letters, printed and widely circulated in the sixteenth century, the idea of a new continent came to be accepted in Europe. If the latter explanation is valid, it is a fitting tribute to the part Italians played in discovering the 'new world' and disseminating information about it.

The Italian contribution was also an economic one. With the growth of trade in the late Middle Ages, merchants from Genoa and other Italian city states had established commercial colonies in the western Mediterranean and Portugal. A large part of the trade with North Africa passed through their hands, and Madeira's production and export of sugar owed much to Genoese finance. As the Black Sea, formerly a major area of Genoese trading interest, declined as an outlet for the overland trade with Asia and then, in the fifteenth century, passed into Turkish hands, Genoese involvement in the western Mediterranean grew. Despite some initial friction, merchants and financiers from Genoa generally operated in close association with Portugal and Castile. A wealthy Genoese financier, Francisco Pinelo, was instrumental in raising funds for Columbus's first and second voyages across the Atlantic; he was rewarded in 1503 by being appointed to the *Casa de Contratacion* (House of Trade) in Seville which supervised commercial transactions between Spain and the New World. Genoese, Florentine and German finance also contributed to the funding of early Portuguese voyages to the Indies: in 1505 the Florentines and Genoese put up 30,000 florins for the large Portuguese fleet that left that year for the East. In return, the Genoese made handsome profits from their capital investments and played a large part in the sale of the spices, sugar and silver that flowed into Lisbon and Seville from overseas.

To a large extent, therefore, the Italians were satisfied with indirect participation in the Age of Discovery. There were other reasons why they did not attempt to take a more direct role. Italian galleys and trading vessels were better suited to the calmer waters of the Mediterranean than to the rougher seas and vast expanses of the Atlantic. A Genoese galley which set out in 1291 to find a sea route to the Indies was never seen again. Thereafter, Italians relied on the more appropriate ships and maritime skills of the Portuguese and Castilians for Atlantic trade and voyaging.

Italy's geographical position, which made it the natural focus for Mediterranean trade and placed it at the crossroads of the trade routes from Africa and Asia, was a disadvantage in an age of Atlantic exploration. Especially among the Venetians, long-established traditions of trade fostered commercial conservatism and a reluctance to adapt to new circumstances. Accustomed for centuries to look to the East for their trade and wealth, the Venetians opposed the expansion of Turkish power in the eastern Mediterranean in a long series of naval clashes between 1499 and 1573. But the Venetians were not bent upon a religious crusade against Islam. They had traded with the Muslim Mamluks of Egypt and Syria in the past and sought to come to terms with the Turks so that the valuable spice trade could be resumed. They were partially successful in this, securing, for example, a temporary agreement with the Turks in 1519. It was once thought that the opening of the Portuguese route to the spice islands had an immediate and permanently damaging effect on the Venetian economy. This is not now thought to be so. By about 1520 the overland spice trade was reviving and Venice again became a major importer and distributor of spices. Portugal's trading costs were high and, it was rumoured, the quality of its spices, impaired by the long sea voyage, were inferior to those from Venice. Partial recovery quietened Venetian apprehensions and discouraged the merchants of Venice from making any substantial adjustments in their traditional pattern of trade. The city owed its long-term decline as much to its general neglect of developing Atlantic commerce as to the Portuguese, and later Dutch, spice trade.

Political and cultural factors further inhibited Italy from greater participation in the Age of Discovery. The courts and city states of Renaissance Italy vied with each other in displaying their wealth and artistic achievement. Conspicuous expenditure at home and aggrandisement within Italy left few resources for expansionist schemes in distant continents. They bred an introspection and complacency that contrasted with the poorer, but correspondingly more adventurous, states of the Atlantic seaboard. The first Atlantic voyages coincided, too, with a period of invasion and armed conflict in Italy. Internally divided, Italy was ill-prepared to resist French and Spanish ambitions in the peninsula and its economy suffered in the resultant warfare. The states of western Europe, by contrast, were emerging as more united and powerful political entities, sufficiently stable and secure at home to be able to experiment with exploration and expansion overseas.

Portugal and Spain

Perched on the southwestern rim of Christian Europe, Portugal was one of the first of the emergent nation states of Europe to stabilize its political boundaries. By the close of the thirteenth century the last Muslim-held territory in the south, the Algarve, had been reconquered, and until 1580 Portugal successfully resisted attempts to incorporate it into a larger Iberian state. Intermittent conflict with Castile, which erupted into open warfare in 1383–1411 and again in 1474–9, served both to strengthen Portugal's sense of its separate identity and to fuel competition between the two states in North Africa and the Atlantic islands. The Treaty of Alcaçovas, which brought to an end the war of succession in 1479, also divided the Atlantic islands between the two rivals with Portugal retaining the Azores and Madeira but being obliged to recognize Castilian claims to the Canaries. The Portuguese capture of Ceuta in 1415 caused concern in Castile, especially as the port lay on the Spanish side of the Strait of Gibraltar. But not until the fall of Granada in 1492 was Castile free to follow Portugal into mainland North Africa.

For a country as poor and as small as Portugal, with little prospect of expanding its territory at the expense of European neighbours, overseas expansion assumed great political and economic importance. Although the great majority of Portugal's inhabitants, numbering about one million at the end of the fifteenth century, were peasants, the land was too poor and rocky to support more than a modest agricultural economy. Portugal lacked the commercial expertise and resources to break into the established trade of the Mediterranean, but it was well placed to participate in the expanding trade between northern and southern Europe, to fish for cod and tunny in the Atlantic and to trade in grain, wine and sugar from the Azores and Madeira, as well as exporting its own olive oil and wine. Its Atlantic location could thus be turned to commercial advantage. The pattern of winds and currents in the Atlantic made Portugal (along with the adjacent Spanish coasts) the ideal point of departure and return for ships trading with the islands or searching the ocean for fish. The maritime and commercial orientation of Portuguese expansion was thus established early on, and contrasted with the predominantly land-based character of Castile's expansion.

Portugal's internal political and social conditions also favoured expansionism. The revolution of 1383–5 brought to power the Avis dynasty, which was generally sympathetic to the aspirations of Portugal's small but growing commercial middle class and which itself saw the economic benefits to be gained from extending Portuguese power overseas. Prince Henry the Navigator, celebrated for the expeditions he sent to explore the West African coast, also promoted the colonization of Portugal's Atlantic islands and the development of their sugar production. Portugal's nobility had reason to share in this enthusiasm for expansion. Since wars of conquest had become virtually impossible at home, they looked to Africa and later Asia for the opportunity to acquire land, wealth and prestigious appointments under the Crown.

Spain, by contrast, had traditionally looked more to the Mediterranean than to the Atlantic. The Aragonese and Catalans of eastern Spain had formerly directed their commercial and political ambitions towards Italy, the Balearic islands and North Africa. The process of unification and national consolidation was also less advanced than in Portugal. The marriage of Ferdinand of Aragon and Isabella of Castile in 1469 and their victory in the war of succession of 1474–9 brought a union of their two Crowns, but the states themselves remained separate, retaining their own laws and institutions. Nevertheless, even this degree of unification freed Christian Spain from the internal divisions that had formerly preoccupied it and gave the country the energy and strength to pursue expansionist policies. Isabella's decision to sponsor Columbus's Atlantic expedition in 1492 was one expression of this new-found confidence.

Like Portugal, Spain had been profoundly affected by the *Reconquista*, the centuries-long struggle to regain the peninsula from the Muslim Moors. The crusading tradition remained a powerful influence on Castilian ideas and attitudes. The vigour with which Isabella followed the defeat of Granada with the expulsion of the Jews, the forcible conversion of the Muslims and the establishment of the Inquisition, is indicative of the queen's determination to root out the non-Christian influences that had been so integral a part of medieval Spain. With only a narrow strait dividing Christian Spain from Muslim North Africa and with Turkish influence in the Mediterranean growing, it was not surprising that Isabella saw overseas expansionism as continuing the fight against Islam, and, in backing Columbus, as the means by which to carry Christianity into 'heathen' lands. Earlier in the century, Prince Henry of Portugal had also seen his expeditions in a similar light. Although the Portuguese wars of reconquest were already more than a century distant when Henry despatched his first ships down the West African coast, he was inspired by the medieval myth of Prester John, believing that somewhere in Africa he would find a powerful Christian prince with whom to ally in a joint crusade against Islam.

Religious motives did not exist in isolation. They reinforced, and were often used to justify, economic and political objectives. Religion in the fifteenth century was a part of everyday life, inseparable from considerations of politics or trade. But the significance of the religious factor is that it gave additional confidence and determination to the expansionism of Portugal and Castile. The intensity of their religious convictions, their profound belief in a divinely authorized mission to overthrow Islam and convert the heathen, led the Portuguese and Castilians into overseas ventures that the more cautious and pragmatic states of Europe, particularly of Italy, would have thought foolhardy and unrewarding. Religion is important, therefore, in explaining why it was the Iberian states that took the lead in overseas expansion.

The *Reconquista* had other consequences, too, for Castilian expansionism. As the Muslims were defeated and the borders of Islam retreated, the newly liberated territories were incorporated into the states of Christian Spain. Christian colonies were established, new towns created. This process of assimilation through conquest and colonization was subsequently repeated overseas in the Canaries and in the Americas. The land-based territorial character of this expansion contrasted with the commercial empires of Genoa and Venice, which consisted of small colonies of merchants located, as at Lisbon, Seville or Alexandria, within the territories of other states, along with a few strategic or commercially important islands, like Rhodes and Crete in the Mediterranean. Portugal's seaborne empire was to fit the Italian pattern far more closely than Castile's rambling land empire in the New World.

The frontier of Christian war and conquest also gave Spain's aristocracy an appetite for acquiring wealth, land and prestige through military exploits and, in contrast with the Portuguese petty nobility, a contempt for trade. This left a large part of the trade of Castile in the hands of foreigners, especially the Genoese. A contempt for manual labour, as well as trade, was to be found even among the poorer Castilians. Francisco Pizarro, who was himself from a peasant background, remarked after his conquest of Peru in 1533, 'I came here to get gold, not to till the soil like a peasant'. Within Spain itself a restless and turbulent frontier spirit had been kept alive by one of the most extensive pastoral economies in Europe. The mobile sheep-herders of Estremadura in western Spain and the cattlemen of Andalusia in the south provided the Spanish *conquistadors* (conquerors) in the Americas with many of their toughest soldiers and settlers. Paradoxically, therefore, the relative economic backwardness of Portugal and Spain and the persistence of the crusading tradition on the Iberian frontier, as well as geographical location, explain why this region, rather than any other in Europe, pioneered overseas expansionism.

Technology and exploration

The Age of Discovery did not represent a clear and immediate break with Europe's past. The motives of many of the leading figures of the age continued to reflect medieval preoccupations – witness Prince Henry's quest for Prester John, Isabella's anti-Muslim crusade, and Columbus's attempt to reach the China and Japan described in Marco Polo's *Travels*. Even when new lands were reached, Europeans' first reaction was to try to incorporate them within the body of information known to them from classical, biblical and medieval texts. Columbus remained convinced until his death in 1506 that he had discovered islands off the coast of mainland Asia, not a New World hitherto unknown to Europe. Early explorers in the Americas imagined themselves transported to a biblical Eden or encountering the peoples and places described in classical mythology or medieval romances. Only gradually did reason and empirical observation prevail over myth, fantasy and fear. And yet, alongside the legacy of the past, the Europeans of the fifteenth and sixteenth centuries displayed a new spirit of enquiry, an ability to adapt and improve on existing maritime technology and to resolve major problems of geography, navigation and ship construction through persistent experimentation.

The Portuguese exploration of West Africa directed by Prince Henry is a striking demonstration of the process of experimentation and learning. As far as Cape Bojador, just south of the Canaries, ships sailed familiar waters: they could hug the African coastline and still find the winds and currents to carry them home. But the unfavourable onshore winds and the rough waters of the cape seemed to confirm sailors' fears that beyond lay an unsailable 'green sea of darkness', an ocean of monsters and boiling brine. In passing Cape Bojador in 1434 and finding a passage back to Portugal by sailing further out into the Atlantic, Prince Henry's navigators broke through the psychological as well as physical confines of medieval navigation and opened the way for the exploration of all the oceans of the world.

The Europeans of the fifteenth and sixteenth centuries could draw upon two navigational traditions to assist them in their voyages – one derived from the East, the other from experience of sailing Europe's own waters. Although the exact process of transmission is difficult to establish, it is known that a number of significant navigational aids originated in maritime Asia. The value of a floating magnetic needle to determine north was probably first appreciated by the Chinese and then spread, via Indian and Arab navigators, to Europe. Through contact with Arab shipping in the Mediterranean Europeans may also have adopted the use of the astrolabe as an instrument to establish a ship's position from the elevation of the sun and stars. It was from the Arabs, too, that Christian Europe acquired the lateen or triangular sail characteristic of Muslim dhows. But in each case Europeans adapted and improved upon navigational aids derived from the East. The magnetic needle, for example, was fixed with a brass pin to a card indicating the principal points of the compass. By the early fifteen century this improved instrument was sufficiently reliable to be the main means of navigation used by ships in the Mediterranean when out of sight of land. Similarly, a modified lateen sail came to be used not simply as a substitute for square sails in European ships, but as an additional means of propulsion alongside them.

Combating the strong seas, winds, currents and vast distances of the Atlantic was a demanding apprenticeship for Portuguese navigators. However, once the Portuguese rounded the Cape of Good Hope and entered the Indian Ocean their rapid progress through maritime Asia was greatly assisted by being able to draw upon the knowledge and skills of Asian pilots and sailors. In 1498 Vasco da Gama sailed directly from the East African port of Malindi to Calicut on the southwestern coast of India with the help of an Indian Muslim pilot familiar with the monsoon winds of the western Indian Ocean. Blowing from the southwest to the northeast from April to August and in the reverse direction from December to March, the monsoon winds enabled direct trade between India and East Africa. Thus, while it took the Portuguese nearly eighty years to pioneer their Atlantic sea route from Morocco to the Cape of Good Hope, helped by Asian navigational expertise and knowledge they were able to reach China in only a further fifteen years.

The adoption of navigational aids and instruments of Eastern origin and the use made of the expertise of Indian Ocean pilots indicate the extent to which the Age of Discovery can be seen as a Eurasian, rather than a purely European, achievement. But Europe's ability to adapt and extend the information and technology received from outside sources and to combine this with its own navigational experience gave it a decisive lead over maritime Asia.

The expansion of seaborne trade and shipping, especially in northern and western European waters, during the late Middle Ages stimulated improved navigational techniques and ship construction, just as the Portuguese experience of Atlantic voyaging was to do in the fifteenth century. The development of a rudder attached to a ship's stern-post gave vessels more reliable steering especially in the strong tides of northern coastal waters. Pilotage in the North Sea and Baltic was aided by the compilation of rutters, written sailing directions, which embodied generations of accumulated knowledge about winds, tides, shallows and coastal features. The Mediterranean equivalent of these written guides became the basis for charts, known as *portolans*, depicting coastal features, ports and navigational hazards. As nautical charts, the *portolans* were still at a relatively primitive stage in the fifteenth century: they treated the sea as a plane surface, for example, and made no allowance for the earth's curvature. But, using the direction lines which radiated from reference points on the charts, navigators could calculate the distance between two points and plot a course to steer between them by dead-reckoning.

While rutters and *portolans* helped pilotage in Europe's frequented coastal waters or in short voyages out of sight of land, they were no use in the uncharted and unfamiliar waters of the Atlantic. There navigation rather than mere pilotage became essential, an ability to sail a course and determine a ship's position without reference to known landmarks. Experimentation and a rational approach to problem-solving were vital in making this possible. By the mid-fifteenth century Portuguese navigators, in passing beyond Cape Bojador, had learnt that by sailing in a large loop (or *volta*) away from the African coast to the northwest they would find the westerly winds to carry them back to Portugal. Familiarity with the North Atlantic *volta* helped the Portuguese when they crossed the Equator and began their attempt to round southern Africa. They gradually realized that the South Atlantic wind system mirrored that in the north, so that to pass the Cape of Good Hope ships had first to sail south-west and then pick up the westerly winds that would carry them eastwards into the

Indian Ocean. This manoeuvre was worked out by Bartholomew Dias in 1486 (or perhaps by now forgotten subsequent expeditions) and it enabled Vasco da Gama in 1497 to sail confidently around southern Africa into the Indian Ocean. In thus moving in a vast sweep across the South Atlantic the Portuguese passed close to South America. They may even have sighted it before Columbus reached the West Indies in 1492. In 1500 Pedro Cabral followed the southern *volta* on the way to India and landed on the coast of Brazil, thereby establishing a Portuguese claim to South American territory. Columbus, too, was a beneficiary of the knowledge of Atlantic winds and currents built up during the fifteenth century. He crossed the ocean from east to west in 1492 following the trade winds, and then returned early the next year by working his way north from the Caribbean against the trades until he found the westerlies to carry him back to Europe.

Sailing the uncharted Atlantic, often at vast distances from the land, also obliged the Portuguese to place greater reliance on their navigational instruments, the compass, astrolabe and quadrant. The difficulty of determining a ship's position in the Atlantic prompted John II of Portugal in 1484 to set up a commission of mathematical experts to devise the best method of finding latitude by observation of the sun. Existing tables of declination, giving the sun's angle above the horizon at different places, were revised and simplified for navigational use. A mathematician was then sent out on a voyage to the West African coast to check the accuracy of the tables by practical observation. Thus exploration and navigational technology progressed hand-in-hand. Long-distance voyaging, in itself encouraged by the development of better navigational aids and ships, presented Europeans with practical problems which they then set out to resolve by experiment and rational problem-solving. Of course, there were many errors and inadequacies. It was not until the eighteenth century, for example, that satisfactory instruments for determining longitude were developed. And for much of the time sailors and navigators continued to rely upon traditional signs to determine the nearness of land – the presence of birds or floating vegetation, the colour of the sea, the character of cloud formations and so forth. Nonetheless, by 1600 major advances had been made in the development of European navigation.

One of the most significant factors behind the fifteenth- and sixteenth-century voyages was the improvement in ship design and construction. Much of the medieval trade of the Mediterranean was carried in slow vessels, with broad, rounded hulls and propelled by one or more lateen sails. Galleys, with their sleek, narrow hulls and driven by banks of oars, were capable of short bursts of considerable speed, but they were better suited for naval warfare or for the transportation of light, high value cargoes, like spices, than for bulk goods such as grain. Galleys were also generally unsuited for the rougher conditions of the Atlantic, though in the fourteenth and fifteenth centuries large Venetian galleys made annual voyages to Flanders and England. Northern European shipbuilders, by contrast, constructed sturdier vessels, known as cogs. These were built for trade in the Baltic and North Sea, carried a single square sail, and (unlike the smoothly jointed and caulked hulls of the Mediterranean vessels) were clinker-built with overlapping planks. The advantage of the cogs lay in their cheapness and their superior cargo-carrying capacity.

Until the fifteenth century northern and southern ships retained separate and distinctive identities. But with the growth of trade between the two regions there began to develop along the coasts of Portugal and southern Spain hybrid vessels that combined characteristics of both styles. The most famous of this new breed of ships was the caravel. This was a small ship, seldom more than 70 tons and 60 or 70 feet in length. It had a straight keel and a stern-post rudder, and carried two or three lateen sails, or, later, a combination of lateen and square sails. Vessels of this kind were probably first developed for local trade around the Portuguese and Spanish coasts, but in about 1440 Prince Henry adopted them for African exploration. Although the caravel had little room below its deck for crew or cargo, its shallow draught made it ideal for exploring close to the shore and in creeks. Its lateen sails enabled it to make use of light winds, to run before the wind or sail close to it. Caravels could also be fast: with a favourable wind, they could cross the Atlantic from the Cape Verde Islands to the Antilles in twenty-one days, a speed barely improved upon until steamships arrived in the nineteenth century. Of the three ships used by Columbus in 1492, two, the *Pinta* and the *Nina*, were caravels.

The third, the flagship *Santa Maria*, was a slower, square-rigged vessel: it proved less suitable for exploration and was abandoned after it hit a reef in the West Indies.

Ideal for exploration, the caravels were less appropriate for longer voyages and for cargo-carrying once the new trade routes had been established, and were seldom used in Portugal's trade with the East. Instead, considerably larger ships, carracks or *naos*, were introduced, broad-beamed, high-sided craft, with three or four decks. Their tonnage rose from about 400 tons in the early sixteenth century to about 1000 tons fifty years later and as high as 2000 in the seventeenth century. They retained a mizzen lateen sail but combined it with a number of square sails to give a greater expanse of canvas. By the late sixteenth and early seventeenth centuries the Dutch and English were beginning to outstrip the Portuguese and the Spanish in the design of specialized fighting and trading ships.

Through the development of its ships and navigational technology in the fifteen and sixteenth centuries Europe was able to turn to advantage its position on the edge of a medieval world stretching from the Atlantic to the China Sea. The once-daunting 'green sea of darkness' became Europe's highway, enabling it to trade directly with Africa and Asia and to gather for its own use the mineral wealth and natural resources of the Americas. Without acquiring a mastery of the seas, Europe might have remained isolated and largely dependent upon its own resources. Against a resistant and resiliant Islam, Christian Europe's latest expansionist drives might have exhausted themselves, as earlier ones had done, in the Holy Land or North Africa. In an age when transport by land remained slow and hazardous, caravels and carracks opened up for Europeans an unprecedented opportunity to explore, to trade and conquer throughout the oceans of the world. It was an opportunity they were not slow to seize.

Africa

The significance of Africa in fifteenth- and sixteenth-century European expansionism is often overlooked. It is too readily seen as a mere prelude to Portugal's discovery of a direct sea route to the

East and of the first trans-Atlantic crossing to the west. In fact the voyages sponsored by Henry the Navigator between 1419 and his death in 1460 had as their objectives the exploration of the African coast and the exploitation of African resources. The possibility of opening up a new route to the spice islands of the East may only have been contemplated by Henry in the last years of his life and was not immediately grasped as a practical objective until the reigns of John II (1481–95) and Manuel (1495–1521).

One of Prince Henry's principal aims in sending expeditions south was to bypass the Muslim traders of North Africa and to establish direct contact with the gold-producing region known to lie beyond the Sahara. For the first twenty years his ships returned to report only a barren coastline with few inhabitants and little prospect of trade. It was only in 1444–5, when an expedition reached the mouth of the Senegal River, that the Portuguese found a more fertile and populous land and evidence of gold.

The Portuguese were, however, to find penetration to the goldfields of the interior impractical. Dense rain-forest divided the coast from the gold-producing areas and the African peoples of the region were able to prevent a Portuguese advance. On land the Portuguese had few of the advantages they enjoyed at sea. Apart from the Gambia, there were no major navigable rivers along which they could sail into the interior. Their firearms, still of a primitive and rather unreliable nature, were often less effective than African spears or bows and arrows. African rulers could mass thousands of warriors: the Portuguese, poor in resources and manpower at home, could muster only a few. Tropical diseases, such as malaria and yellow fever, caused high mortality among their soldiers and sailors. They were forced, therefore, to remain at the coast and rely upon African intermediaries to bring gold to them in exchange for European and North African goods, like copper and textiles or for beads and slaves traded elsewhere on the Guinea coast. In this way the Portuguese succeeded in diverting part of the former Saharan gold trade to the coast. In the late fifteenth and early sixteenth centuries West Africa yielded about 400 kilograms of gold a year for the Portuguese. More to protect this trade from European rivals than from African rulers (on whose goodwill and self-interest they were heavily dependent), the Portuguese constructed a series of coastal forts. They included Arguin, begun in 1445, Elmina (the principal outlet for gold from the Akan forest) in 1482 and Axim in 1503. These fortified trading stations were the prototype of the European 'factories' later established in Asia and the Americas.

In southeastern Africa in the early sixteenth century the Portuguese discovered a second gold trade, one of which they had previously been unaware. This ran from the region of present-day Zimbabwe to the coastal cities of Sofala and Kilwa. Through the bombardment and partial destruction of these sites and the creation of their own base on Mozambique island, the Portuguese succeeded in diverting part of the gold trade into their own hands. They also penetrated a few hundred miles along the Zambezi valley, but, as in West Africa, failed to establish control over the actual gold-producing area.

Apart from gold, the Portuguese at first traded in other African products, such as ivory and West African pepper, but their interest in these declined once they reached the Indies, which they saw as a much wealthier and more rewarding trading area. East Africa retained its importance to the Portuguese as a supplier of gold for trade in Asia and as protecting the western flank of their Indian Ocean empire. In the west of Africa, the only other trade apart from gold that was of lasting interest to the Portuguese was that in slaves. At first these were seized by raiding along the coast, but by the 1480s they were being obtained as part of Portugal's commerce with African states and traders. During the fifteenth century most of the slaves were transported to Lisbon to be sold: an estimated 150,000 were taken to Europe between 1450 and 1500. With the opening up of the Americas, particularly the establishment of sugar plantations in Portuguese Brazil in the late sixteenth century, the slave trade switched direction and grew in volume.

The profitability of the slave trade, along with the allure of Guinea gold, also attracted other Europeans to the West African coast. Sir John Hawkins began England's involvement in the trans-Atlantic slave trade in 1562, but it was the Dutch who, from the 1590s, presented the most serious threat to Portugal's position on the coast. In the 1630s the Dutch seized several Portuguese trading ports along the West African coast: Portugal regained the Angolan slaving ports of Luanda and Benguela, but Elmina and Axim in the Gulf of Guinea were lost to them forever.

Though predominant, commerce was not Portugal's only concern in Africa. Hostility to Islam was a continuing feature of Portuguese relations with northwest and eastern Africa, and the destruction of the predominantly Muslim cities of Sofala and Kilwa owed something to the religious fervour of the Portuguese as well as to their commercial ambitions. A Portuguese emissary in search of Prester John reached the Coptic Christian kingdom of Ethiopia as early as 1494, but further contacts were slow to develop. Four hundred Portuguese soldiers were sent to help the Ethiopians resist a Muslim invasion in 1541–3, but the close alliance that Prince Henry had once dreamt of still failed to materialize. Ethiopia was less powerful than medieval European fantasy had portrayed it. Portuguese and Ethiopian interests had little in common: even their forms of Christianity were very different.

Elsewhere in Africa the Portuguese made intermittent efforts to convert African rulers and to Christianize and Europeanize their peoples. The most celebrated example of this was in the Kongo Kingdom which lay to the south of the Congo River. Missionaries, teachers and craftsmen were sent out from Portugal in the 1490s and in 1506 a Christian convert ascended the Kongo throne as Affonso I. He favoured closer ties with Portugal, but with the opening up of the Indies trade Portuguese interest rapidly dwindled. An opportunity for creative and peaceful contact was lost and the Kongo kingdom was turned over to the slave traders. Portugal's economic interests in Africa triumphed at the expense of its religious idealism.

Asia

At first sight at least, the Portuguese achievement in Asia was a remarkable one. Within little more than fifty years after Vasco da Gama's arrival at Calicut in southwest India in 1498, Portuguese seapower spanned the Indian Ocean from Mozambique in East Africa to Malacca on the Malayan peninsula; it extended to Hormuz on the Arabian Gulf and Macau off the coast of southern China. For many historians the arrival of the Portuguese marked a decisive break with Asia's past. The Indian historian K. M. Panikkar wrote of a 'Vasco da Gama epoch' beginning in 1498 and ending with the collapse of European empires in Asia after the Second World War. From a European perspective other historians have emphasized the apparent ease with which the Portuguese established themselves in Asia, though their explanations for this vary. Some stress the effectiveness of Portuguese ships and cannon. G. B. Sansom attributed Portuguese achievements to their 'spirit of determination to succeed, which was stronger than the will of Asian people to resist'.

We have already seen the limitations of Portuguese power in Africa, despite their advantages at sea. Was it really the case that the Portuguese had such a sudden and dramatic impact on Asia that, in the words of J. H. Plumb, 'the Orient lay at Europe's mercy'?

Nowhere in Asia did the Portuguese establish for themselves a land empire like that of the Spanish in the Americas. It is unlikely that they ever even aspired to. Their primary interest was in creating and maintaining a profitable maritime empire. They had neither the resources in men and arms nor the motive to try to seize and retain vast territories. Instead, in pursuit of their commercial objectives, the Portuguese took advantage of rivalries between local powers to form alliances with princes who were prepared to trade with them or fight on their behalf. When the Zamorin of Calicut (ruler of that part of southwest India with which the Portuguese first made contact) refused to meet their demands, the Portuguese turned instead to his neighbour and nominal vassal, the Raja of Cochin. Having secured a base further north at Goa in 1510, the Portuguese were able to develop trade and a military alliance with the Hindu rulers of the Vijayanagar empire of south India. Asia, like Africa, failed to present a united commercial and military front to the Portuguese intruders. Alliances such as these could serve to protect Portuguese interests on the coast and extend their influence inland, but they did not create for the Portuguese a territorial dominion of their own. Moreover, such alliances were often unreliable: princes changed sides or dragged the Portuguese into unwanted wars.

It was at sea that the Portuguese enjoyed their greatest advantage. Before their arrival in the Indian Ocean naval battles had been rare and trade was generally conducted peacefully between the different racial and religious communities. Asian ships were designed for trade, not war. Apart from some Chinese junks, they were seldom large and their construction – of overlapping planks held together with coconut rope rather than iron nails – was weaker than that of the Portuguese vessels. Accustomed to European waters, where armed conflict at sea had become common, Portuguese ships carried cannon – da Gama's fleet of 1498 had twenty guns – and they were not reluctant to use them. Muslim ships were attacked and destroyed, coastal forts and towns bombarded. In 1509 the Portuguese scored a decisive victory over a Gujarati-Egyptian fleet off Diu in western India and they were not again seriously challenged in the Indian Ocean until the arrival of the Dutch and English almost a century later. There were reverses – the Chinese worsted the Portuguese at sea in 1521 and 1522 – but on balance Portuguese ships and guns made them the dominant power in maritime Asia.

That there was conflict at sea shows that Asians did not meekly accept Portuguese mastery but struggled to oppose it. At first they did so by open defiance. Subsequently, once the strength of Portuguese ships and cannon had been demonstrated, they more often did so by evading Portuguese controls. The maritime ascendency of the Portuguese was helped by the lack of interest of many of Asia's greatest states in naval power and seaborne trade. The Chinese empire of the Ming dynasty, the Vijayanagar state in south India, the Mughal empire established in northern India in 1526 – each saw itself as essentially a land empire, drawing its wealth from the soil and from internal trade rather than from maritime commerce. Vijayanagar's rulers valued trade with the Portuguese, especially the horses they brought from Hormuz, but the Mughal and Ming emperors saw the Portuguese as largely irrelevant to their own domestic concerns, and thus made no attempts to oppose them directly.

As in Africa, the initial aggressiveness of the Portuguese owed something to their religious convictions. It was religiously unacceptable for them to settle down to trade peacefully alongside Muslims, even if it was commercially possible. The intolerant spirit of the *Reconquista* was imported from the Iberian peninsula to the Indian Ocean. But although the Portuguese at first showed considerable aggression against the Muslim traders and princes they encountered in the East, they made only feeble attempts to win Asia over to Christianity. The arrival of the Jesuits at Goa in 1540 brought a more determined religious spirit to Portuguese relations with Hindus as well as Muslims in India; but, outside their own small colonies and with the exception of a few successes like the conversion of the Parava fishermen of southern India in 1537, the Portuguese came to accept that, in the interests of trade, they had in practice to tolerate the established religions of Asia, even Islam.

Religious considerations apart, the Portuguese resorted to the use of force to establish themselves in maritime Asia because they could not otherwise attain their commercial objectives. Trade in the Indian Ocean operated on a complex network of regional exchanges. Different areas produced different goods. Textiles from India, for example, were a major item of trade with East Africa where they were exchanged for gold and ivory; they were traded, too, with the Indonesian islands in return for spices. Apart from copper from Europe and gold from Africa, the Portuguese had no valuable trading goods to contribute to this trading system, as Vasco da Gama discovered when he tried to buy spices at Calicut in 1498. Muslim resentment at the arrival of Christian traders in a region they had hitherto dominated added to the difficulties of the Portuguese in establishing themselves commercially. Force, therefore, appeared necessary to break into the Asian trading world.

Under Afonso de Albuquerque, Governor of the Portuguese Indies from 1509 to 1515 and often seen as the real architect of Portuguese power in the East, a twofold system of maritime and commercial control was developed. The first part consisted of seizing and holding a small number of strategically or commercially important sites from which it would be possible, even with Portugal's limited resources, to dominate the most valuable trade routes. Goa, taken in 1510, became the centre of Portugal's trade with India and its administrative capital in the East. In the west, in addition to Mozambique and Mombasa on the East African coast, in 1515 the Portuguese took Hormuz, an island commanding the approaches to the Arabian Gulf. They failed, however, in 1513 and 1548 to capture Aden, which would have given them command of the Red Sea. Attempts to use their fleets to block Muslim trade with the Red Sea met with no more than limited success. In the east, Malacca was taken in 1511: this was the main collection point for spices from the Indonesian islands and the meeting place of Indian Ocean and Chinese trade. Further east, the Portuguese occupied a number of the spice-producing islands, notably the Moluccas, the main source of nutmeg, mace and cloves. They advanced, too, into the trading system of the China Sea, establishing bases at Macau for trade with China in 1557 and at Nagasaki in Japan.

The second part of the Portuguese bid for commercial control was the introduction of a system of passes (*cartazes*). Issued by Portuguese harbour officials, these permitted Asian vessels to carry approved cargoes along specified routes. The measure was a further curb on Muslim trade and freedom of movement through the Indian Ocean region. But, more substantially, it was designed to secure for the Portuguese a monopoly in certain valued products, especially pepper, and to enable them to tax other trades and Asian shipping. The passes were also an attempt to enforce Portuguese claims to sovereignty over maritime Asia.

Having established themselves by force, the Portuguese settled down to the profitable exploitation of their commercial empire. In addition to maintaining the trade in spices to Europe that had been their original objective in the East, the Portuguese also became deeply involved in the carrying trade of Asia and this proved to be particularly lucrative, especially for Portuguese merchants and officials in the East. Portuguese ships, for example, maintained a valuable trade from China to Japan, via Macau and Nagasaki, in gold, silver and silks. Through their participation in Asia's carrying trade the Portuguese assimilated themselves to the pre-existing pattern of trade and only partly succeeded in imposing upon maritime Asia a distinctively European trading system. In commerce, as in religion, the Portuguese impact was a significant but restricted one.

The Portuguese empire in the East had fundamental weaknesses that made it vulnerable through both internal decay and external assault. From the handful of bases envisaged by Albuquerque at the beginning of the sixteenth century, the number had steadily increased as new areas of trade were opened up or renewed attempts were made to plug the gaps in the system of maritime control. By 1600 there were some fifty forts between East Africa and Japan. Portugal, poor even in European terms, could not hope to maintain such a large number of far-flung possessions, to run them at a profit and to defend them from attack. The problem of distance was in itself a formidable obstacle to effective commerce and administration in the East. While it took only three weeks to cross the Atlantic, the voyage to Goa was seldom accomplished in less than six months. A return journey from Goa to Macau or Nagasaki and back might take from eighteen months to three years. Losses of ships on these long voyages were heavy, especially between Lisbon and Goa in the late sixteenth and seventeenth centuries, and further taxed the profitability of the empire.

The greatest external challenge came from European rivals, principally the Dutch. Exploratory trading voyages financed by Dutch merchants in the 1590s were quickly followed by the founding of the Dutch East India Company in 1602. Over the course of the following sixty years the Dutch wrested from the Portuguese many of their most lucrative trading posts, especially in the spice islands. The triumph of the Dutch was not merely a military and naval one. It was also commercial. The Dutch were rapidly emerging as Europe's foremost trading nation. They already held a major share of the European carrying trade and had the world's largest mercantile marine. They thus possessed the ships, the commercial expertise and the capital resources to operate an Asian trading empire more efficiently and profitably than the Portuguese pioneers.

America

European exploration and expansion in the Americas present a strikingly different picture from those in Africa and Asia. It was there that the arrival of the Europeans had its greatest and most enduring impact. Instead of developing trade with the indigenous population, the Europeans established territorial empires and began to settle in the Americas themselves. By 1600, when the Portuguese empire remained no more than a string of islands and forts from West Africa to China, the Spanish had already acquired in the Americas a domain many times the size of Spain. Why was there such a contrast between the two empires?

The explanation lies partly in the different forces behind Spanish expansionism, to which attention has already been drawn (p. 18), and partly in the very different conditions to be found in the Americas. As we have seen, the Portuguese empire was a seaborne and commercial one, growing out of Portugal's traditions of maritime trade and Atlantic seafaring. The traditions and outlook of Castilian Spain were significantly different.

When Columbus approached the Portuguese court in 1484 with his plan to sail westwards across the Atlantic to Japan and China, the Portuguese had two reasons for rejecting him. Firstly, they were already heavily committed to African exploration and trade and were about to make their long-desired breakthrough to the Indian Ocean. They were not inclined to postpone grasping the known wealth of Asian trade for the uncertain returns of a western voyage. Secondly, their geographical knowledge was sufficiently advanced for them to appreciate that Columbus had wildly underestimated the circumference of the globe and hence the distance west from Europe to Asia. By contrast, the Spain of Isabella of Castile was a relative newcomer to Atlantic exploration. As late starters and as rivals of the Portuguese, the Castilians had little to lose and perhaps much to gain by sponsoring Columbus.

The new land mass revealed by Columbus's expeditions was at first an unwelcome obstacle to Spanish ambitions to find a westward route to Asia. A way was sought around or across it. There was some curiosity about the new continent's size and extent, but more impelling to Castile was a fierce sense of rivalry with other powers. The Portuguese were known to be advancing rapidly across maritime Asia; by 1500, they had landed on the Brazilian coast of South America. Through the voyages of Cabot, the English were also showing an interest in the western continent, though little of practical consequence followed from this apart from the exploitation of the Grand Banks off Newfoundland by fishermen from Portugal, England and France.

Competition with the Portuguese was made keener by a series of papal bulls and treaties attempting to fix a line of demarcation between Spanish and Portuguese interests. The Treaty of Tordesillas in 1494 drew an imaginary line 370 leagues west of the Cape Verde islands to divide Columbus's discoveries in the west from Portugal's African claims to the east. The line was in fact drawn so far west as to permit the subsequent Portuguese claim to Brazil. A papal bull issued in 1514 by Leo X granted to the Portuguese not only such lands as they might seize in Africa and India but also territory in any region they might reach by sailing east. This spurred the Spanish to try to reach the spice islands by their westerly route before the Portuguese could establish themselves there from the Indian Ocean.

From their forward bases on the Caribbean islands of Hispaniola and Cuba the Spanish despatched expeditions to search for a route through to the East Indies. In 1513 Vasco Nunez de Balboa, a local Spanish commander, crossed the narrow neck of land that forms the isthmus of Panama and reached the Pacific coast. The narrowness of the continent at this point gave encouragement to the hope that a convenient route might be found around America and across the Pacific. In order to test this possibility, an expedition under Ferdinand Magellan, a Portuguese in the employment of Castile, set out from Seville in September 1519. Magellan, who had been present at the Portuguese capture of Malacca in 1511 and may have visited the Moluccas, was convinced that the spice islands lay close to the western shores of Spanish America. The expedition sustained great hardship and loss in discovering that this was not in fact the case. Magellan himself was killed in a clash with islanders in the Philippines in 1521 and the voyage back to Europe was completed by his Spanish second-in-command, Sebastian del Cano. The three-year voyage, the first circumnavigation of the globe, demonstrated that the only way around South America lay too far south and was too perilous to be a regular commercial route. It revealed, too, that the Pacific Ocean was considerably wider than Magellan had anticipated. It took his starving, desperate crews nearly four months to cross, during which time they sighted only two small islands. The voyage dramatically advanced European knowledge of the far side of the world and incidentally established a Spanish claim to the Philippines. But it convincingly demonstrated that America formed an almost impenetrable barrier and that sailing west from Europe would not provide Spain with a route to the spice islands to rival Portugal's.

Even before the voyage of Magellan and del Cano had shown America's remoteness from Asia, the Spanish had begun to see the new continent as more than an inconvenient obstacle and to view it instead as a potentially abundant source of wealth and power. One attraction was the prospect of land. The restless, land-hungry frontier of the Spanish *Reconquista* crossed the Atlantic first to the Caribbean and then to the American mainland. With it came the demand for labour to work the land, for the Spanish conquerors and settlers, contemptuous of manual labour had no desire to till the soil themselves. Through the grant of *encomiendas* by the Crown of Castile, leading settlers were given the right to the labour of the Indians of specified villages. African slaves were soon introduced to increase the supply of available labour or replace the Indians who died or were killed during the early phase of Spanish colonization.

In the Americas, as in Asia and Africa, the Spanish and Portuguese ignored the rights of indigenous peoples to the land they occupied, maintaining that only Christians could have a valid title. In Africa and Asia the Portuguese seldom attempted to translate such claims into actual possession. But in the Americas, following the precedent of the Spanish *Reconquista*, European settlement became a characteristic form of expansion from the outset. Columbus, in his second voyage in 1493, brought 1200 Spaniards, including farmers and craftsmen, to settle on the Caribbean island of Hispaniola, where they were expected to become a self-sufficient community, look for gold and prepare for the further extension of Spanish control in the region.

In the vanguard of territorial expansion in the Americas were the *conquistadors*. These professional conquerors and adventurers sought wealth and land for themselves, though they claimed to act in the name of the Spanish monarchs. Their personal sense of destiny was reinforced by the strength of their belief in their religious and moral superiority over the Indians. Bernal Diaz, chronicler of the Spanish conquest of Mexico, summed up the *conquistadors'* aims as being 'to serve God and His Majesty, to give light to those in darkness, and also to get rich'.

The *conquistadors'* greatest hope of becoming rich was by acquiring gold, the most tangible and desirable form of wealth and power they could imagine. Columbus had returned to Spain in 1493 to report that he had seen evidence of gold in the islands and expected to find much more. This prospect, as with the Portuguese in Africa, was the most powerful of all incentives to further exploration. Within twenty years of Columbus's first voyage all the main islands of the Caribbean had been stripped of their gold. Significant quantities were found, but the Spanish appetite was insatiable and they turned their attention to the mainland. Here they were encouraged by hearing of wealthy civilizations in the interior and of 'El Dorado'. Although the expression has come to mean a land of fabulous wealth, at the time of the explorers and *conquistadors* it referred to a 'gilded man', a King who reputedly covered his body in gold dust in an annual ceremony before bathing in a sacred lake. Once again myth, rather than reality, shaped the character of European expansion. A frantic search for gold accounts for both the rapidity and the rapacity of Spanish exploration and conquest in Central and northern South America. Between 1520 and 1550 Spanish adventurers crossed the Andes and sailed down the Amazon, penetrated into the north of present-day Argentina and Chile, and investigated Florida and the lower Mississippi basin. They failed to discover vast quantities of gold, but by their searches they rapidly sketched in the geography of the region on Europe's maps.

A quest for gold, land and personal glory lay behind the Spanish conquests of Mexico and Peru. In 1519 an expedition of about 600 men under Hernando Cortes arrived on the Gulf coast of Mexico from Cuba. It made its way by warfare, diplomacy and bluff from the coastal jungles to the high plateau of central Mexico and the Aztec capital, Tenochtitlan (the site of today's Mexico City). Despite their small numbers, the Spanish took the emperor Montezuma captive, overwhelmed Aztec forces in the capital and finally, in August 1521, defeated Montezuma's successor to establish Spanish rule in central Mexico. The remarkable success of

Cortes and his soldiers prompted a second *conquistador*, Francisco Pizarro, to lead an even smaller force of about 150 men against the Inca empire in the Andes of Peru in 1531. Within two years the Inca emperor, Atahualpa, had been captured and executed and his empire annexed to Spain.

How were such small numbers of Europeans able to conquer such vast and populous empires? The Spanish, unlike the Portuguese in Africa and Asia, did not find in the Americas existing trading systems which they could take over or partially control. Although for a brief period they bartered beads for gold on the Gulf coast, it was the rumoured wealth of the interior that attracted them, the prospect of conquest and plunder, not a restricted coastal trade. Moreover, despite their small numbers the invaders were confident in the superiority of their religion and European civilization. This gave them an often reckless determination to succeed.

The indigenous peoples of Central and northern South America were ill-prepared technically and psychologically to resist determined European invasion. Although the Mexicans' stone-edged swords and fire-hardened arrowheads could inflict fatal wounds, they were not comparable to the steel swords and cannon of Cortes's force. These, with the Spaniards' horses (animals previously unknown in Mexico), helped the invaders to victory in several important skirmishes. The psychological advantage of guns and horses was greater than the purely military. Their possession served to alarm the Indians and shake their confidence in their own ability to win. Montezuma himself was uncertain how to respond to the Spaniards, whether to treat them as dangerous enemies to be kept at the greatest possible distance or as the gods they were rumoured to be. Cortes skilfully played upon the emperor's indecision, defying his orders to remain at the coast, then at Tenochtitlan befriending him and trapping him into becoming a virtual puppet ruler in the hands of the Spanish. Other factors, like the outbreak of an epidemic of smallpox, a disease unwittingly introduced by the Spanish to Mexico, further enhanced the invaders' advantage by demoralizing the Indians and causing them to doubt the power of their own gods against the Spaniards' Christ. The speed of the invasions of Mexico and Peru and the vast technical and cultural gap between the Europeans and the native Americans gave the latter no time to recover from the shock of European intervention, no time to devise effective methods of resistance against them, to acquire horses and guns to use against them. When, much later, the North American plains Indians took up both these innovations, they showed that they could be used with considerable effect against the settlers and soldiers of the United States.

The invaders were also able to exploit two basic weaknesses in the Aztec and Inca empires. Because these were centralized states under a single emperor, by capturing the person of the emperor and seizing the imperial capitals the Spanish *conquistadors* could in effect capture or at least temporarily paralyze the power of the state. The second weakness was that, in expanding their territory into more distant areas, the Aztecs and Incas had created discontented subjects or hostile adversaries on the borders of their empires. These could readily be won over by the invaders, like the peoples of coastal and eastern Mexico, to become military allies or porters, guides and spies. The acquisition of indigenous collaborators compensated for the Spaniards' own numerical weakness; and through them they acquired information about the country and its people that enabled them to fight their principal enemies more effectively. In Peru, the Incas' capacity to resist Spanish invasion was further undermined by a recent civil war and Atahualpa's still uncertain hold over the empire.

The age of the *conquistadors* was dramatic and destructive but shortlived. From their bases in Mexico and Peru the Spanish began the lengthier task of subjugating the other peoples of Central and South America. In some cases this took many decades to achieve. The *conquistadors* squabbled and fought among themselves for the spoils of conquest, but it was the Crown of Castile that was the principal beneficiary. It was not prepared to see a powerful and semi-independent nobility establish itself in the New World as it once had in Spain. In 1535 a Spanish viceroy was appointed and the beginnings of an imperial administration created. Although the search for El Dorado continued fitfully, Spanish America settled down to more stable occupations. The Indians' cultivation of maize, potatoes and other vegetable crops was threatened by the introduction of large-scale ranching from Spain's own pastoral frontier. The demoralized Indians who survived the conquest were greatly reduced in numbers through disease and compulsory labour. The population of central Mexico is estimated to have fallen from 25 million at the time of the conquest to barely one million by 1600. The conquest and the rigorous suppression of traditional forms of worship enabled Christianity to advance more rapidly than in Africa and Asia. Between 1524 and 1536 about 4 million conversions were recorded in Mexico alone.

Although the *conquistadors* had been disappointed in their dreams of El Dorado, in the 1540s the Spanish discovered silver in abundance at Potosi in present-day Bolivia and at Zacatecas in Mexico. Silver, not the gold that had inspired exploration and conquest, rapidly became the real American mineral bonanza. Apart from its effects, by no means all beneficial, on Europe's own economy, the silver enabled the expansion of Europe's trade in spices and textiles from Asia. The age of a European world economy was dawning.

Conclusion

Historians today are less inclined than those in the past to see the Age of Discovery in terms of a sudden breakthrough in European technology or as the achievement of a few individuals who, almost single-handed, pioneered oceanic exploration. Rather they see the voyages and the conquests of the fifteenth and sixteenth centuries as the outcome of economic, cultural and technological developments that had been maturing within Europe since at least the eleventh and twelfth centuries. To say this is not to deny individuals any importance. The imagination, daring and determination of men like Prince Henry, Dias, da Gama, Columbus, Magellan, Cortes and Pizarro accelerated the pace of European expansionism and helped to determine its character and direction. But they built upon or pushed to new limits existing European knowledge, skills, resources and ambitions. If Columbus had not crossed the Atlantic in 1492, if Cortes had not seized Mexico in 1521, it seems certain that other European navigators and adventurers would have done so sooner or later.

In the voyages of the Vikings, the wars and conquests of the Crusaders, and the commercial activities of the Genoese and Venetians, Europe had made preliminary attempts at expansionism. These had failed to develop into fully-fledged expansionism because before the fifteenth century Europe had lacked the navigational technology, the resources and the sustained motivation for systematic exploration and expansion overseas. What was distinctive about the Age of Discovery in the fifteenth and sixteenth centuries was the combination of Iberian initiative and more general European involvement. Portugal and Castilian Spain provided a crusading zeal unique to themselves; they constituted an ideal geographical location for oceanic exploration. But Europe as a whole, with Italy in the lead, contributed expertise in navigation and cartography, essential financial support, and markets for the spices, gold and other goods brought back to Europe in Iberian ships. The specifically Iberian factors made Portugal and Castile the pioneers of expansionism, but, after 1600, other European states, especially Holland, England and France, were to sustain and extend the expansionist process.

In seeking to explain why the European Age of Discovery occurred when and as it did, modern historians have looked at other civilizations to try to understand why these did not anticipate, match or prevent European expansionism. There is now much greater awareness than formerly of the relative narrowness of the technological gap between Europe and China, India and the Muslim world in the fifteenth and sixteenth centuries. And even in Africa and the Americas, where the technological gap was clearly greater, historians write with far less confidence about the advantages European ships and firearms enjoyed over indigenous peoples. It is now apparent that in many parts of the world Europeans lacked the material power and resources to impose their will upon others.

In essence, Europe's advantages were threefold. Its expanding economy and the importance attached to trade gave to its overseas ventures a sustained motivation and determination. Experience of warfare and political rivalry within Europe, combined with intermittent conflict with Islam, gave an additional confidence and aggressiveness to Europe's voyagers and adventurers. Few if any states outside Europe possessed such a powerful combination of economic motivation and religious-cultural self-righteousness. It was this combination that constituted Europeans' 'determination to succeed' often in spite of adverse conditions. China, perhaps the greatest of Europe's potential rivals, was by contrast largely content with its own economic and cultural self-sufficiency. This bred a contempt for external trade and foreign peoples, not European-style commercial and cultural aggression. To Europe's distinctive motivation was added a developing spirit of enquiry and a rational approach to problem-solving. Superstition, fantasy and deference to the authorities of the past were not dead, but they were more than matched by a European capacity to investigate geographical, navigational and technical problems and to discover, through trial and error, practical solutions to them.

Armed with these basic assets, Europe was able to exploit local situations as it found them. In some areas, like the Americas, Europeans had the advantage of surprise in their assault on indigenous societies. In the Indian Ocean there was less surprise and more effective opposition, but Europeans found local rivalries to exploit, seized bases and won naval victories that gave them enough of a foothold to pursue their commercial and political ambitions. Through persistence and opportunism these initial bridgeheads were gradually extended. Where Portugal in Asia lacked the resources fully to exploit its achievements, the Dutch and English stepped in after 1600 to develop their own commercial and territorial empires.

The period 1400 to 1600 was thus one of reconnaissance, of oceanic exploration, the opening up of new trade routes, and the beginnings of overseas empires. After 1600, in the hands of the Dutch and English in particular, maritime exploration assumed less importance than the consolidation of established trade routes and the development of new ones. The gold and spices that had first tempted Portuguese ships beyond the stormy waters of Cape Bojador were joined, and to some extent superseded, by a new commerce in slaves, sugar, silver, calicoes, coffee and tea. The wealth thus derived from overseas trade helped to finance or to prompt further empire-building in the Americas and Asia. It also contributed, directly and indirectly, through the further development of capitalism and the Industrial Revolution, to the western imperialism of the nineteenth and twentieth centuries which left hardly any part of the inhabited globe untouched. The process of European exploration and conquest, once set in motion in the fifteenth century, had, by the first half of the twentieth, become a truly world-wide phenomenon.

Recommended reading

C. R. Boxer, *The Portuguese Seaborne Empire, 1415–1825* (Harmondsworth, Penguin, 1973).

P. Chaunu, *European Expansion in the Later Middle Ages* (Amsterdam, North Holland Publishing House, 1979).

J. H. Parry, *The Age of Reconnaissance: Discovery, Exploration and Settlement, 1450 to 1650* (Berkeley, University of California Press, 1981).

J. H. Parry, *The Discovery of the Sea* (Berkeley, University of California Press, 1981).

J. H. Parry, *The Spanish Seaborne Empire* (Harmondsworth, Penguin, 1973).

G. V. Scammell, *The World Encompassed: The first European maritime empires, c. 800–1650* (London, Methuen, 1981).